WORSHIP FOR EVERYONE

A Journal For All Ages

NICK & BECKY DRAKE
AND PERRY-MAY BRITTON

First published in Great Britain in 2021

Worship for Everyone
www.worshipforeveryone.com

ISBN 979-8-492-26316-4

The Team: Eloise Akehurst, Simon Baker, Becky Drake, Nick Drake, Noah Drake, Perry-May Britton

Illustrations by Perry-May Britton
Cover design and typesetting by Simon Baker, Thirteen Creative

CONTENTS

WEEK 3: CITY ON A HILL – LET YOUR LIGHT SHINE 45

WEEK 4: MASTERPLAN – THERE IS NO-ONE LIKE YOU! 63

SALVATION PRAYER 80

WELCOME!

One of the most important things in all the world is...

Talking to God every day.

Why?

Because then you're reminded of his love in you, his presence with you, and his purposes for you.

Living life each day with God is just... better!

We've created this journal to help you do that every day. Having somewhere to write your prayers and thoughts about God is so helpful, especially if it has Bible verses, ideas and songs in it too!

Whatever your age or stage of life, this journal is for you. You can do it on your own, or work through it with someone younger or older than you and help each other get to know God more!

HOW TO USE YOUR JOURNAL

Each week follows a different theme from the Bible with an accompanying Worship for Everyone song. Read the introduction, and then throughout the week you can listen to the song either on your own or with others asking God to encourage you and strengthen you as you worship along.

Each day there are several ways that the journal will help you to connect with God around the week's theme.

1. **You'll read a Bible verse and write in the journal.**
    There'll be a few things to read to get you thinking and then some open space to use however you like! Tell God how you feel, draw a picture, write a prayer, make it long or short, bullet points or poetry – whatever you feel like doing! It's just between you and God.

2. **There is always space to write down three things you want to thank God for.** They can be big or small, boring or exciting. You don't need to always fill in all three – sometimes you could instead pick one but write three reasons why. The Bible says that it's good to praise God and that everything we have is a gift from him.

3. **You'll spot each day that there's a little section called 'Noah's Fact'!** Noah is one of Nick & Becky's children and part of the Worship for Everyone team. He loves and remembers all sorts of information and each day he shares a fascinating fact that ties in with the theme. It's so you can learn about the world as you journey closer to our creator God!

4. **Finally, we've included an optional idea or activity that will help you go a bit deeper with the theme.**
    Often it's our actions, no matter how small, that help us to remember what we've learnt or what God is saying throughout the day. Feel free to use the actions or prayers we've suggested, or make up your own.

MAKE THE TIME

Choosing to spend time like this with God can be hard work at first, but you won't regret it if you stop and make time! It doesn't need to take long. How about you set yourself a challenge of doing this journal for four weeks and see how you feel at the end? Our hope and prayer is that you feel closer to God and stronger in your faith. If you miss a day or two, don't worry – that's totally normal. Just pick it up again and keep going!

ONE LAST THING...

If you are in a family setting, you might want to have a copy for each member of your family to do separately, or you might prefer to do one journal but together in pairs or as a group. We're all different. Either way, try and talk together throughout the week about what you've been journalling. That way, we can encourage each other as we go!

Enjoy journalling with God!

Perry-May, Nick, Becky and Noah!

WEEK 1: SLINGSHOT JOURNEYING WITH DAVID

There is no one more powerful than God. He is able to do things through you that you wouldn't think were even possible!

Here's something amazing: you can talk to God at any time about things that worry you or feel scary or overwhelming. His power can fill you, and help you to face the things you're afraid of. By asking for God's power in your life (his Holy Spirit), you can be an amazing blessing to your friends, family and the world! People will begin to be amazed and surprised by what God does in and through your life.

This week we are looking at the story of David and how God's power worked through his life. You might know the story of David and Goliath already. God's people (the Israelites) were at war with the Philistines. Among the Philistine army was a huge man (described in the Bible as a giant called Goliath) who said he would take on any member of the Israelite army, and if they beat him they would win the entire battle! No one would do it. But then, a young shepherd boy – David – came along and offered to face the challenge. Through his faith in God, together with a few stones and a slingshot, he actually managed to defeat the scary Goliath!

As we start, we'll read together the words he said to the Philistines just before he flung his first stone at Goliath.

LISTEN TO THE SONG
Scan the QR code to listen now!

Or visit **worshipforeveryone.com/song/slingshot**

Day 1

MIGHTY GOD

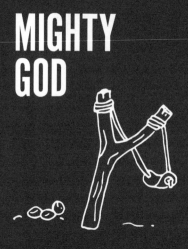

All those gathered here will know that it is not by sword or spear that the Lord saves: for the battle is the Lord's, and he will give all of you into our hands.

1 SAMUEL 17:47

The story of David and Goliath is pretty wild isn't it? A tiny shepherd boy used his little slingshot to knock down a man the size of a giant! This big enemy, Goliath, had terrified an entire army – but not little David!

What's wild is that Goliath wasn't only fighting David. Goliath was fighting 'God in David'. And it's pretty obvious that God's going to win that battle every time. There is no-one like him!

This same God is in you today. Let that sink in. God is alive and living in you by his Holy Spirit. The Bible tells us in 1 John 4:4: 'greater is he that is in you than he that is in the world'. God is greater than any 'giant' or power we have to face. In fact, when we rely too much on our own strength, we can end up feeling really tired.

We also end up missing out on God's power. The best thing we can do is tell God when we feel weak and ask God to be 'the power in me'. He's the one who'll take on the battle for us – just like he did for David.

Write down a list of anything that feels too big or scary. You might be starting a new school or a new job. You might be scared of the dark. There might be people you feel scared of. When you've finished, write in big letters THE BATTLE IS THE LORD'S.

TODAY I'M THANKFUL FOR...

1. _____

2. _____

3. _____

_____

_____

_____

_____

_____

_____

_____

_____

_____

_____

NOAH'S FACT

The biggest ever slingshot was created in Norway. It was 4.56 metres across, which is about as tall as a London bus!

Go outside today and find a couple of stones. Hold them in your hand. Maybe even pop them in your pocket for the day! All David had was five small stones and a homemade slingshot. Remember that list of all the scary things in your life? Imagine the power of God in those little stones, knocking down the giant Goliath. Ask God for that same power to fill your life today.

Day 2

MIGHTY ME

Small but mighty!

Don't let anyone look down on you because you are young.

1 TIMOTHY 4:12

David was the youngest in his family. Each day his mum would send him off with a whole stack of packed lunches for his big brothers who were fighting in the Israelite army. But David couldn't fight because he was too young.

Where do you fit in your family? Are you the oldest? The youngest? Have you ever felt small because of your height or your age? Other things can also make us feel 'small'. Sometimes people don't treat us well. Sometimes we just don't feel very confident. David felt small too.

Many years later, Timothy was another young person who felt small. Paul, his older friend, tells him in our verse today not to let this hold him back. Throughout the Bible, God used a lot of young people to do incredible things: David, Joseph, Esther... even Mary was only a teenager when she carried God's own son. Never rule yourself out because you feel small. God loves working with people just like you.

Write down any areas of your life where you feel small or lack confidence. Now take a pen and draw a big cross over it, as a way of saying today that this is not how God sees you. Now write down three positive things about yourself. Perhaps some way you're good at loving other people, one of your talents ,or something else you like.

TODAY I'M THANKFUL FOR...

1. _____

2. _____

3. _____

_____

_____

_____

_____

_____

_____

_____

_____

_____

_____

NOAH'S FACT

The smallest mammal in the world is the bumblebee bat, which weighs only two grams and measures around one inch in length – about the size of a large bumblebee.

Pray this prayer: *'Father God, thank you that throughout the Bible you often use the youngest or shyest or most surprising people to do amazing things! Help me to know how special I am to you and to be bold enough to step out in faith today. Amen.'*

Day 3

WORSHIP IS KEY

The heavens declare the glory of God, the skies proclaim the work of his hands.

PSALM 19:1

David spent his time looking after sheep. Often he was on his own – just him and God in nature. David would have watched the sun rise and set again and felt the rain on his face in the fields. He'd have seen lambs born and spring come, then winter hit the land as he snuggled down with his sheep to keep warm.

When we spend time in nature, our hearts are filled with wonder. Nature is one of the gifts from God that helps us respond to him. And the more we wonder, the more we worship!

It makes sense then that David was an amazing worshipper. He became famous – not only for using his slingshot against Goliath, but also for his worship of God. He wrote many songs and poems to God, like today's verse. He recited these in the fields as he looked after the sheep. He played the harp and he danced in worship. For David, worship was key to living each day with God.

Write down or draw some of your favourite places to be outside. Maybe places near your home, or places you've been on holiday. Where do you feel most happy or inspired when you're outside? The sea? The fields? In the park? Mountains? A sunny sky?

TODAY I'M THANKFUL FOR...

1. _____

2. _____

3. _____

_____

_____

_____

_____

_____

_____

_____

_____

_____

_____

NOAH'S FACT

On Earth there are seven times as many trees as there are stars in the Milky Way galaxy.

Go outside today and thank God for your favourite places and for all he has made. Notice the small things around you in nature and thank God for each of them: a flower, the grass, a tree, a bird. Spend time praising him.

Day 4

A HEART LIKE DAVID

Create in me a
pure heart and
renew a steadfast
spirit within me.

PSALM 51:10

The Bible tells us that David was a man 'after God's heart' – in his heart he longed for the same things that God does.

What is your heart after? What does it long for? What do you spend your time thinking about, wishing for, working on? Take a moment to jot down honestly some of the things your heart wants.

What would it look like if your heart was more after God's heart? Which of these things would you cross off your list? Which things maybe seem less important now?

David asked for a pure heart. Pure means having only one thing, one substance in it. Just like a glass of pure water – it's pure because it's not contaminated with anything else! A pure heart is a heart that is full of God's love. Nothing else.

List now some of the things God is passionate about. A great place to start is love. That's his golden rule – anywhere that we see love in action, God is happy! Where could your heart line up more with his? Ask the Holy Spirit to line up your heart with God the Father's. Ask for a pure heart like David does.

TODAY I'M THANKFUL FOR...

1. _____

2. _____

3. _____

_____

_____

_____

_____

_____

_____

_____

_____

_____

_____

_____

NOAH'S FACT

Love Heart sweets were invented for Swizzels by David Dee in 1954, and were originally only found in Christmas crackers.

Turn on the tap and wash your hands. As you see the water flowing, ask the Holy Spirit to give you a heart like God's heart. A heart that cares for the things he cares about. A heart that is pure, and full of love. Ask him to remove anything impure, and make you more like Jesus.

Day 5

INFLUENCER

faith popping out
of me!

David served God's
purpose in his own
generation.

ACTS 13:36

What do you want to do when you grow up? And if you're already grown up, what are you doing right now?

We all want our lives to make a difference, to truly know that we have served God and fulfilled his plans for our lives.

When we choose to give our lives completely to God, we can have peace and confidence that he won't waste us! In fact, he will use us in the most remarkable ways, just like he did with David. We will have a deep sense of purpose!

Draw a picture of yourself or write out your name in big bubble letters. Give your life again to God today. Now write down the phrase 'full of faith' near your name.

Make that your prayer today – that you will be willing to do anything, go anywhere and serve God in whatever way he calls you. It may be that you need to make a minor change to what you're already doing, or it may be something big in your future! Each step of faith adds up!

TODAY I'M THANKFUL FOR...

1. _____

2. _____

3. _____

_____

_____

_____

_____

_____

_____

_____

_____

_____

_____

NOAH'S FACT

In a recent survey of UK children, the most desired job was to be a doctor or nurse, and 3% of children wanted to be Prime Minister!

Take a quiet moment to think about what you're hoping for – the dreams and passions you have in your heart to serve God. It's never too early or too late to give them to God. Don't be shy about naming these out loud honestly to him. Leave them in God's hands, trust him, and see what happens.

Day 6

PEACE BRINGER

Whenever the spirit
from God came on
Saul, David would take
up his harp and play.
Then relief would come
to Saul; he would feel
better, and the evil spirit
would leave him.

1 SAMUEL 16:23

Music is a gift from God. It's a mysterious and amazing thing! It can make us happy and excited, or sad and reflective. It can drive an entire room to dance! It can send us to sleep.

David was a musician. He sang and wrote songs. He also played the harp. In fact, he ended up being King Saul's personal harpist! David was the only one who could soothe Saul with his playing. When David played the harp, the Bible even says evil would be overcome and Saul was able to sleep in peace.

David used his musical talent to bring peace to others. Where could you carry peace into the world? Write down the name of someone who needs to know God's peace. Write down the name of a country that needs peace. Or something in creation that needs peace. Let God speak into your mind as you write and pray for this person or this situation. Ask God to help you to be a peace-bringer.

TODAY I'M THANKFUL FOR...

1. _____

2. _____

3. _____

_____

_____

_____

_____

_____

_____

_____

_____

_____

NOAH'S FACT

Music improves your memory. It can reduce the body's level of cortisol which makes you stressed, and with less stress you will learn better and remember more!

Find a worship song or a piece of music that soothes you and speaks to you. Sit and listen to the music. Use the time to pray for God's peace to settle your own heart, just as he brought calm to Saul. If you have peace, you can bring peace to others.

Day 7

IMPERFECT ME, PERFECT GOD

David said to Nathan 'I have sinned against the Lord.' And Nathan said to David, 'The Lord also has put away your sin.'

2 SAMUEL 12:13

David wasn't perfect! In fact, he did some pretty bad things. Despite being a worshipper, a king and a faith-filled warrior, he also had at least eight wives over the years, and he even plotted to kill people!

God doesn't look for perfect people. In fact, there aren't any perfect people anywhere. Can you imagine how guilty David must have felt when he'd messed up? Many of his psalms show us just how bad David felt. In Psalm 51, David says: 'I know my sin is always before me.' But God never stopped forgiving him and never stopped using him, as Nathan reminded David in today's verse.

Write down the word 'forgiven' in the middle of the page. You can make it big or small.

Look at that word and say, 'I am forgiven'. Take a moment to write anything that pops into your mind where God has forgiven you. It can help to write down specific things you feel guilty about and then put a line through them to remind you that they are gone.

Now write the name of Jesus on your page. Nothing stands in the way of God using you because of what Jesus has done on the cross!

TODAY I'M THANKFUL FOR...

1. _____

2. _____

3. _____

_____

_____

_____

_____

_____

_____

_____

_____

_____

_____

NOAH'S FACT

In a recent survey of names associated with good behaviour at school, those called Noah came in second place, topped by boys called Arthur! In the girls category, Isla and Ava came out on top.

Take a moment to reflect. Is there anyone you need to forgive today? Just as God forgives us, he wants us to forgive others. Allow God to bring to mind anyone who you need to forgive, and ask God to help you to let go of any hurt they may have caused.

Well done on completing Week One: Slingshot!
Never forget that God loves working with people
who feel weak or small like little David!

God's power is always available for people like you.
Don't count yourself out of doing anything. If God
calls you, God will equip you. Trust in him and don't
let your own worries hold you back from stepping
up into his plans and purposes for your life!

THINGS I'VE LEARNED ABOUT GOD THIS WEEK

_____

_____

_____

_____

_____

_____

THINGS I'VE LEARNED ABOUT ME THIS WEEK

_____

_____

_____

_____

_____

_____

_____

WEEK 2:
EVERY STEP
YOU ARE
NEVER ALONE

I am full of God's love.

One of the great themes throughout the Bible is God's wonderful promise to always be with us.

He was with Adam and Eve in the very beginning, Joseph when he was thrown into the bottom of the well by his brothers, Moses and Miriam as they worshipped in the desert after God had saved them from Egypt, and many more Old Testament characters. But then, in Jesus, God himself came to live with us on Earth! Jesus is alive today and with us by the Holy Spirit. The Spirit is God's special presence, who helps us live our lives each day following in Jesus' footsteps.

This week we are going to look at how God loves to guide us, lead us and walk every day with him.

LISTEN TO THE SONG
Scan the QR code to listen now!

Or visit worshipforeveryone.com/song/every-step

Day 1

GOD IS WITH US

'She will give birth to a son, and you are to give him the name Jesus, because he will save his people from their sins.'

All this took place to fulfil what the Lord had said through the prophet: 'The virgin will conceive and give birth to a son, and they will call him Immanuel' (which means 'God with us').

MATTHEW 1:21-22

Do you have more than one name? Or a nickname that you are often called?

Jesus had many names and they all had a special meaning. One of his names was Immanuel. Immanuel means 'God with us'. Right from the beginning of time God had a very special plan to make sure that we would not be on our own. Jesus, God's Son, was sent to be with us.

Write about a time when you may have felt lonely or sad and then ask God to show you where he was in that moment. It is wonderful to know that, even though you may have felt alone, he was actually there with you.

TODAY I'M THANKFUL FOR...

1. _____

2. _____

3. _____

_____

_____

_____

_____

_____

_____

_____

_____

_____

_____

_____

_____

_____

_____

_____

NOAH'S FACT

In a recent study of names, more people choose baby names beginning with the letters on the right side of a computer keyboard. Names like Olivia, Noah and Liam are now more popular than ever!

Use a Bible or the internet to find out some of the names that God or Jesus has (for example, 'Jehovah Jireh' means 'God who provides'). Pick one of them and memorise it. What does it mean to you? You could also think about the names you are called or names you call others. Our names really do matter!

Day 2

GOD GUIDES OUR STEPS

How sweet are your
words to my taste,
 sweeter than honey to
my mouth!
I gain understanding
from your instructions;
 therefore I hate every
wrong path.

Your word is a lamp for
my feet,
 a light on my path.

PSALM 119:103-105

It is a wonderful thing to know that it is very hard to take a wrong turn with God because he has given us the Bible, his word. His word is tasty – sweeter than honey!

The Bible is like having a big torch when you are walking in the dark. God loves to guide us and show us which is the best path for us to take.

Do you have any tricky decisions to make? Are you wondering what you should do about a friendship or something else in your life? Write about it here, or draw a picture of the situation and then ask God to show you, by his Holy Spirit's power, what he thinks about it! Maybe a few Bible verses or a passage of scripture will come to mind, or maybe just a sense of peace and his presence with you.

TODAY I'M THANKFUL FOR...

1.

2.

3.

_____

_____

_____

_____

_____

_____

_____

_____

_____

_____

_____

_____

_____

NOAH'S FACT

The average person walks 65,000 miles in their lifetime – that's three times around the Earth!

Find a quiet spot and grab your Bible and something sweet – maybe a spoon of honey or a sweet. As you experience the sweet taste, thank God for sending his Son and giving us his sweet word to guide us.

Day 3

NOTHING CAN SEPARATE US

For I am convinced that neither death nor life, neither angels nor demons, neither the present nor the future, nor any powers, neither height nor depth, nor anything else in all creation, will be able to separate us from the love of God that is in Christ Jesus our Lord.

ROMANS 8:38-39

My wise midwife said to me when I gave birth to my oldest child, 'children need three things – food, sleep and unconditional love.'

Well, these three things are not just important for newborn babies, they continue to be important throughout our entire lives. We don't just need food to grow, we need a constant source of love to grow *well*. And today's beautiful verses from the book of Romans remind us that nothing at all can ever separate us from God's love. God being 'with us' means God's love is forever with us.

Imagine God speaking to you today. Write down what you think he would say to you. Think of some of the ways he would encourage you, build you up and pour out his love into your life. Read your words back. They are a letter of love coming from your Father.

TODAY I'M THANKFUL FOR...

1. _____

2. _____

3. _____

_____

_____

_____

_____

_____

_____

_____

_____

_____

_____

_____

NOAH'S FACT

Animals with the strongest family bonds include elephants, wolves, orcas, dolphins, lions and chimpanzees.

Just for today, try attaching something to your clothes or putting something in your pocket that you don't normally have – like a sticker, a badge, or a ribbon. Throughout the day, use this as a reminder that God's love is stuck to you forever. Every time you notice it, give thanks to God for his unconditional love.

Day 4

WALKING WITH GOD

Ooo! I've got butterflies!

When he was at the table with them, he took bread, gave thanks, broke it and began to give it to them. Then their eyes were opened and they recognised him, and he disappeared from their sight. They asked each other, 'Were not our hearts burning within us while he talked with us on the road and opened the Scriptures to us?'

LUKE 24:30-32

The two disciples were walking to the village of Emmaus when the risen Jesus came to walk with them. They didn't recognise him, but their hearts were burning within them as he walked with them along the road and spoke about God's word.

Often when God speaks to us or is very close we can feel a lovely warm feeling in our hearts or even our tummies. It can be like having butterflies or an excited sense of anticipation, or it can be a sense of deep peace, knowing everything is going to be okay.

Walking with Jesus is always an adventure. It's one of the most exciting things you could do. You never know where he will lead but you know it will be the right place for you and the best place for you to be a blessing to other people.

It might be that today you decide to commit to walking with him for the rest of your life (you could use the prayer on page 80). Or it may be that you know you haven't been walking very closely with him and you make a choice to draw near again. Or perhaps you just need to remember that he is right there, walking beside you. Write down your response to God today.

TODAY I'M THANKFUL FOR...

1. _____

2. _____

3. _____

_____

_____

_____

_____

_____

_____

_____

_____

_____

_____

NOAH'S FACT

The word 'walk' comes from the word 'wealcan' which is an old English word and literally means 'to roll'.

Go for a walk and invite Jesus to walk with you. Have a chat with him on the walk, tell him whatever it is you want to tell him and ask him to speak to you. It's a very simple form of prayer and when you start chatting with Jesus regularly you will find your heart 'burning' within you quite often!

Day 5

WAITING FOR A GIFT

On one occasion, while he was eating with them, he gave them this command: 'Do not leave Jerusalem, but wait for the gift my Father promised, which you have heard me speak about. For John baptised with water, but in a few days you will be baptised with the Holy Spirit.'

ACTS 1:4–5

We know that God sent his Son, Jesus, to be with us, but he also had another gift for us. Jesus told his disciples to wait for the gift that God the Father had promised. It was the gift of the Holy Spirit.

One of the names of the Holy Spirit is the 'Paraclete'. It is a Greek name and it means someone who is 'called alongside', a little bit like a coach running next to an athlete or a teacher full of encouragement. The teacher helps the student be the best they can be. Write down one or two ways you would like the Holy Spirit to help you today.

Can you think of anything you have been waiting for – maybe a birthday or even Christmas? What does it feel like to wait? How would you feel about waiting for the Holy Spirit to come and fill you up? Write 'I'm waiting for you' and make that your prayer today.

TODAY I'M THANKFUL FOR...

1. _____

2. _____

3. _____

_____

_____

_____

_____

_____

_____

_____

_____

_____

_____

NOAH'S FACT

An average person spends 52 days of their lives waiting in a queue.

Make something, or do something today you don't normally do – it could be baking a cake, trying a new sport, or a new idea you have at work. As you do it, imagine the Holy Spirit (the Paraclete) coming alongside you, encouraging and helping you. God is right there with you and he is delighted to be with you in whatever activity you do. He is clapping and cheering you on.

Day 6

RECEIVING THE GIFT

When the day of Pentecost came, they were all together in one place. Suddenly a sound like the blowing of a violent wind came from heaven and filled the whole house where they were sitting. They saw what seemed to be tongues of fire that separated and came to rest on each of them. All of them were filled with the Holy Spirit and began to speak in other tongues as the Spirit enabled them.

ACTS 2:1-4

It must have been very exciting on the very first day that God's Holy Spirit came and filled the disciples. It doesn't always happen in such a noisy way!

Have you experienced being filled by the Holy Spirit? What was it like and what difference did it make? Very often when we are filled with the Holy Spirit we are filled with boldness to tell others about Jesus! If you're not sure or don't think you have experienced the Holy Spirit, maybe now is the time to ask him to fill you. Either way, write a prayer asking God to fill you up afresh today.

When someone offers you a gift there is no point in saying, 'thank you very much,' but not taking it or opening it. If you have prayed a prayer to ask God to fill you up, the best thing you can do is put your hands out, just like when you are receiving a present, and say 'thank you, Lord'.

TODAY I'M THANKFUL FOR...

1. _____

2. _____

3. _____

_____

_____

_____

_____

_____

_____

_____

_____

_____

_____

_____

NOAH'S FACT

The largest gift ever given was the Statue of Liberty, which France gave to the USA in 1886.

Ask God to fill you up, and then wait and see what happens. The Holy Spirit might make you feel warm inside, he might make you a bit shaky, he might make you feel a bit emotional... whatever happens just keep saying 'thank you, Lord' and when you are done you may find you feel different inside or maybe you will have become much more courageous or have a peaceful feeling inside. These are all little signs that he is with you.

Day 7

GOD IS FAITHFUL

'As I was with Moses, so I will be with you; I will never leave you nor forsake you. Be strong and courageous, because you will lead these people to inherit the land I swore to their ancestors to give them.

'Be strong and very courageous. Be careful to obey all the law my servant Moses gave you; do not turn from it to the right or to the left, that you may be successful wherever you go. Keep this Book of the Law always on your lips; meditate on it day and night, so that you may be careful to do everything written in it. Then you will be prosperous and successful.'

JOSHUA 1:5-8

In the Old Testament, Joshua was an ordinary person – just like us – and God had a special plan and purpose for him. Joshua had to be strong and courageous, he had to keep his Bible (the book of the Law) very close to him and God promised that he would be with him wherever he went.

God has a special plan and purpose for you too. It may not be to conquer different lands or lead a great number of people, but whatever he has called you to will be very important to God. One really important part we can play is to keep reading his word, being filled with his Spirit, and chatting to him. Know that he is faithful and he will always be with you wherever you go.

Ask God today to give you a few ideas of what he wants you to do in your life. Read today's Bible passage over a few times and then let your heart be glad that he is going with you wherever you go.

TODAY I'M THANKFUL FOR...

1. _____

2. _____

3. _____

_____

_____

_____

_____

_____

_____

_____

_____

_____

NOAH'S FACT

The Bible is the best selling book of all time. It sells 25 million copies a year!

Write a letter to your future self, reminding yourself of what God has spoken to you about over the last few days, weeks, or months. Then write at the bottom: 'Thank you God that you are with me, every step I go'.

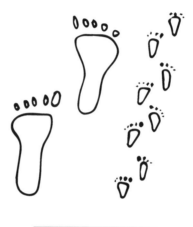

Well done on completing Week 2: Every Step!
God is always with you, no matter what you feel
like or what your circumstances are. His presence
guides you, and will lead you whenever you ask
him. It may not always be obvious, but that's part of
learning to trust him and follow him.

Finally, don't forget that it is God's love that you
need in order to fully grow into who he has made
you to be. His love for you is never-ending and
unbreakable. Enjoy his love for you and be a person
who shares that love with everyone you meet!

THINGS I'VE LEARNED ABOUT GOD THIS WEEK

_____

_____

_____

_____

_____

_____

THINGS I'VE LEARNED ABOUT ME THIS WEEK

_____

_____

_____

_____

_____

_____

_____

WEEK 3: CITY ON A HILL
LET YOUR LIGHT SHINE

Right from the start, God wanted us to shine with his light and life to other people.

He has designed us to be a blessing to our friends, our neighbours and our world. He sent Jesus to show us how to shine and to give us the ability to shine to the full! When we talk daily with God in prayer, get to know his word (the Bible) and ask for his Holy Spirit to fill us, we shine from the inside out with his goodness!

This week we're exploring this theme. Each of us on our own can be a bright torch for God, lighting up the path for others. But put us together and we are a mighty light, shining with hope – a *city on a hill.*

LISTEN TO THE SONG
Scan the QR code to listen now!

Or visit **worshipforeveryone.com/song/city-on-a-hill**

Day 1

GROWING LIGHT

When Jesus spoke to the people, he said, 'I am the light of the world. Whoever follows me will never walk in darkness, but will have the light of life.'

JOHN 8:12

Without light there is no life! Have you ever tried growing cress in a dark cupboard? It's an experiment most of us do at some point. The cress ends up bent, yellow and certainly not fit for eating. Cress needs light!

Light brings life to our planet. And Jesus brings life to us. When we turn towards him and follow his example, our hearts and minds begin to grow healthily. We start to think like Jesus thought and feel the same love for others that Jesus felt. We literally grow stronger and more tasty!

Write down the areas of your life where you feel most alive. What are the things that bring you to life? What brings you joy?

Now think about the darker areas. Where are the sadnesses, worries and disappointments? Where do you need Jesus to shine his light and bring new life to you? Ask him to shine his light on you today and bring life.

TODAY I'M THANKFUL FOR...

1. _____

2. _____

3. _____

_____

_____

_____

_____

_____

_____

_____

_____

_____

_____

NOAH'S FACT

Over one million Earths could fit inside the Sun!

Eat a crunchy apple or juicy peach today and take a moment to think of the light that has fed this fruit. As you eat it, imagine Jesus shining his bright light of life into every area of your mind and body.

Day 2

SHINING LIGHT

'You are the light of the world—like a city on a hilltop that cannot be hidden. No one lights a lamp and then puts it under a basket. Instead, a lamp is placed on a stand, where it gives light to everyone in the house. In the same way, let your good deeds shine out for all to see, so that everyone will praise your heavenly Father.'

MATTHEW 5:14-16 (NLT)

Have you ever looked at a city at night time? Or at a row of houses or a tower block near where you live? When the sun has set, the lights of the buildings still shine in the darkness. They have their own beauty as they glisten in the night, reminding us of life inside the dark walls.

Jesus' light and life lives in you and me. He doesn't want this to be a secret. In fact, it's important to God that we go on shining night and day, announcing to the world that Jesus lives in us! How can you shine with God's love today?

Write down the things that stop you shining. Everything you can think of. Tiredness? Hunger? Busyness? Fear of what people will think or say? Worry?

TODAY I'M THANKFUL FOR...

1. _____

2. _____

3. _____

_____

_____

_____

_____

_____

_____

_____

_____

_____

_____

_____

_____

_____

_____

_____

NOAH'S FACT

The highest city in the world is El Alto in Bolivia, which is 4,150m above the sea!

Now take a moment to reflect on one thing that could help you to shine more today. Do you need to rest? Do you need to walk and pray? Do you need time with someone? Make a decision to do it!

Day 3

THANKFUL LIGHT

Do everything without grumbling or arguing, so that you may become blameless and pure, 'children of God without fault in a warped and crooked generation.' Then you will shine among them like stars in the sky as you hold firmly to the word of life.

PHILIPPIANS 2:14-16

Do you think it's possible not to grumble or complain about anything? Could you manage that?

We're not talking about honestly expressing our sadness, grief or worries – it's very important that we can do that! But grumbling is more about our attitude when things aren't perfect.

Do traffic jams, queues in shops, spilt milk and broken toys send you into a big rant and rave? Or are you able to keep shining, as Paul urges the church in Philippi to do?

Did you notice that Paul suggests that not complaining means that we will shine like stars? All around us people moan about everything from the weather to the price of groceries, to homework and work emails. It's so easy to moan. But what would the church look like if we were known as a group of people who didn't complain or grumble?

Take time today to express gratitude. This is a great way to stop ourselves complaining. Look at all you have and pour out our thanks and praise to God for the many blessings in your life today. Start with the three things you are thankful for at the top of the page and then keep going – write as many things as you can!

TODAY I'M THANKFUL FOR...

1. _____

2. _____

3. _____

_____

_____

_____

_____

_____

_____

_____

_____

_____

_____

NOAH'S FACT

Research shows that most people complain once a minute in a typical conversation. That's a lot of complaining!

Pray that the Holy Spirit will stop you from grumbling or complaining. Ask him to remind you of this verse every time today you're tempted to moan. Let's see how we feel when we turn complaints back to gratitude!

Day 4

GUIDING LIGHT

By day the LORD went ahead of them in a pillar of cloud to guide them on their way and by night in a pillar of fire to give them light, so that they could travel by day or night.

EXODUS 13:21

Light doesn't only *give* life. It also guides us into life. Many years ago, God sent Moses and his tribe, the Israelites, on a long mission through the desert from slavery to the promised land of Canaan. With no torches or devices for light, God himself shone in the darkness in the form of a fire that Moses and his people could follow. God lit up the road ahead for Moses and he will light up our paths too!

Are there areas of your life where you need heavenly guidance today? We can make some decisions for ourselves, but others need a fire by night to shine in the darkness.

Draw a lighthouse. If that feels tricky, draw a big sunshine! Inside it, write anything that feels unclear and in need of direction.

TODAY I'M THANKFUL FOR...

1. _____

2. _____

3. _____

_____

_____

_____

_____

_____

_____

_____

_____

_____

NOAH'S FACT

Originally lighthouses were lit with open fires, using whale oil as fuel.

Ask God to be like a lighthouse or sunshine to you, shining so that you can journey in the right direction each day. Every time you see a source of light today, ask God to guide your life.

Day 5

STRONG LIGHT

What shall we say in response to these things? If God is for us, who can be against us?

ROMANS 8:31

All the way through the Bible, people faced difficult times. God's people always had enemies. When we choose to follow Jesus we have to expect that there will be times when things feel hard and don't always make sense, and sometimes people won't like us because of our faith.

But we can have confidence that God is not just *with* us, he is *for* us. God is on our side, fighting for us, encouraging us, loving us.

Write down what it means to you that God is *for* you. In which area of your life do you most need to know that right now?

TODAY I'M THANKFUL FOR...

1. _____

2. _____

3. _____

_____

_____

_____

_____

_____

_____

_____

_____

_____

_____

_____

_____

_____

_____

NOAH'S FACT

A laser beam one billion times brighter than the Sun has been created in a lab, making it the brightest ever light produced on Earth.

Listen to the song 'City on a Hill' (scan the code on page 45) and praise God that because he is *for* you, you can shine confidently and not be afraid of standing out and speaking up for Jesus.

Day 6

FILLED WITH LIGHT

Jesus is the Light!

'Your eye is the lamp of your body. When your eyes are healthy, your whole body also is full of light. But when they are unhealthy, your body also is full of darkness.'

LUKE 11:34-35

What's your favourite sweet? Have you ever been into a really good sweet shop? The ones where jars of sweets fill the room from floor to ceiling? All across the counters are penny sweets, lollipops and sticks of rock... It's sweet heaven! In a shop like that, it's hard to focus on just one thing. Your eyes go wandering everywhere from one jar to another. What will you choose? How will you decide?!

That's okay if you're in a sweet shop, but not so great if you're driving on a road, or trying to get a piece of work done. Our eyes need to focus. It really matters what we look at, and what we focus on. It'll help to either bring light or darkness to our lives.

Write the name of Jesus at the top of your page today. Look at his name. It's Jesus we need to focus on. He is the light of the world. Write down what you love about him, some of his qualities, some of the things you're grateful for. Today, simply be focused on who Jesus is.

TODAY I'M THANKFUL FOR...

1. _____

2. _____

3. _____

_____

_____

_____

_____

_____

_____

_____

_____

_____

_____

NOAH'S FACT

Your eyes can focus on 50 different objects every second.

Find somewhere quiet today and set a timer for three minutes. During that time, focus on Jesus and ask him to speak to you. Enjoy the stillness. Try not to let your mind drift – stay focused and let him fill you with his love and his presence.

Day 7

LIGHT IS WISDOM

The unfolding of your words gives light; it gives understanding to the simple.

PSALM 119:130

Have you ever heard anyone talk about having a 'lightbulb moment'? It's another way of saying 'I suddenly realised something!' or 'It suddenly made sense!'

The Bible is a source of light. It gives us God's wisdom, which means that the more we read it, the more we understand who God is and what he's like. It helps us to grow a bit wiser, like him, too. As we read the Bible we'll probably find we have all sorts of lightbulb moments!

Today, grab a Bible, turn to the Psalms, and pick one to read (if you're unsure try Psalm 100). Ask the Holy Spirit to be with you as you read it. Write down any words or verses that stand out or speak to you.

TODAY I'M THANKFUL FOR...

1. _____

2. _____

3. _____

_____

_____

_____

_____

_____

_____

_____

_____

_____

_____

_____

_____

_____

_____

_____

NOAH'S FACT

If you travelled at the speed of light, you could travel around the Earth more than seven times every second!

Now that we've spent a week thinking about light, think about someone in your life that needs to experience the love and light of Jesus. Think of one way you could shine a light into their life. Could you write a letter to them, buy them a gift, bake them some treats, pray for them, or something else? Commit to shining your light on them this week.

Well done on completing Week 3: City On A Hill! You were designed to shine with the light of Jesus on everyone you meet. Never hide your light or be ashamed of following Jesus.

As we've seen this week, his light offers so many amazing things to people. It is a light to grow in, a light to guide our lives, and a light to be thankful for. Jesus living in you can change the world!

THINGS I'VE LEARNED ABOUT GOD THIS WEEK

_____

_____

_____

_____

_____

_____

THINGS I'VE LEARNED ABOUT ME THIS WEEK

_____

_____

_____

_____

_____

_____

_____

WEEK 4:
MASTERPLAN
THERE IS NO-ONE LIKE YOU!

You are unique

It's an incredible thing to realise that there is no-one like you.

Only you can be you! This is because God has made you completely unique – with your own fingerprints, your own face, your own thoughts, feelings and dreams. Amazing things happen when we learn to be super confident in who God has made us to be and what he wants to do through us.

This week is all about learning this truth. We'll be journeying with one of the songs contained in the book of Psalms. It's a beautiful poem to God and was written by someone who truly knew God not only as their creator but also as a very close companion and friend.

LISTEN TO THE SONG
Scan the QR code to listen now!

Or visit **worshipforeveryone.com/song/masterplan**

Day 1

KNOWN

You have searched
me, Lord,
 and you know me.
You know when I sit
and when I rise;
 you perceive my
thoughts from afar.
You discern my going
out and my lying down;
 you are familiar with all
my ways.
Before a word is on my
tongue
 you, Lord, know it
completely.

PSALM 139:1–4

It's a wonderful thing to be known. When you are in a crowded place and you hear your name called out, your ears often hear it even above other loud noises.

We naturally long to be known and to belong and it is a wonderful thing that God knows us so completely. Today, write down how you feel about the Lord knowing your thoughts and your words before you speak them.

Then, write down anything you'd specifically like God to know today.

TODAY I'M THANKFUL FOR...

1. _____

_____

2. _____

_____

3. _____

_____

_____

_____

_____

_____

_____

_____

_____

_____

_____

_____

_____

_____

_____

_____

_____

_____

NOAH'S FACT

The Norwegian word for 'know' is 'vet'.

Think about the community that you are in – your family, your friends, your school or workplace. Are there any people God wants you to pray for by name? Make an effort today to speak to others using their names and take an interest in their lives. It will make them feel known and accepted and as if they belong. It will make a difference to you as well!

Day 2

PROTECTED

You hem me in behind
and before,
 and you lay your hand
upon me.
Such knowledge is too
wonderful for me,
 too lofty for me to
attain.

PSALM 139:5-6

God wants us to feel safe. He protects us like a bodyguard, always at our side.

Life won't always be easy but we can feel great comfort in knowing that we have God around us, like a strong set of armour.

Are there times when you know you need him to lay his hand upon you? Write a prayer inviting God to go behind and before you and ask him to specifically put his hand on you in areas of your life that you find challenging.

TODAY I'M THANKFUL FOR...

1. _____

_____

2. _____

_____

3. _____

_____

_____

_____

_____

_____

_____

_____

_____

_____

_____

_____

_____

_____

_____

_____

_____

_____

━━━━━━━━━━━━━━━━━

NOAH'S FACT

The most protected person on earth is the Russian president, who has over 3,000 bodyguards.

━━━━━━━━━━━━━━━━━

Draw yourself surrounded by guards and then remember that God's guards are actual angels! Psalm 91:10-11 says: 'no harm will overtake you, no disaster will come near your tent. For he will command his angels concerning you to guard you in all your ways...' Turn your drawing into a prayer and add some cool angel wings to your guards!

Day 3

ALWAYS WITH ME

God playing hide and seek

Where can I go from
your Spirit?
Where can I flee from
your presence?
If I go up to the
heavens, you are there;
if I make my bed in the
depths, you are there.
If I rise on the wings of
the dawn,
if I settle on the far side
of the sea,
even there your hand
will guide me,
your right hand will
hold me fast.

PSALM 139:7-10

Imagine what it would be like playing hide and seek with God... It would be almost impossible because he would always know where you were hiding! He also only seems to hide sometimes to give us the joy of finding him.

Jeremiah 29:13 says: 'You will seek me and find me when you seek me with all your heart.' Write about the day you first found Jesus and what it felt like to be found or rescued by him. If you are only just discovering him now, why not copy out the prayer on page 80 and make it your prayer today.

TODAY I'M THANKFUL FOR...

1. _____

   _____

2. _____

   _____

3. _____

   _____

_____

_____

_____

_____

_____

_____

_____

_____

_____

_____

_____

_____

_____

_____

NOAH'S FACT

The largest ever game of hide and seek involved 1,437 people and was played in China on New Year's Day in 2014.

Thank God that he is always with you, even when sometimes you can't feel it. Wherever you go today, imagine there is another person walking, sitting, and living your day with you – the presence of God in Jesus. Try talking to him about little things as you go!

Day 4

NIGHT IS LIGHT TO GOD

If I say, 'Surely the
darkness will hide me
and the light become
night around me,'
even the darkness will
not be dark to you;
the night will shine like
the day,
for darkness is as light
to you.

PSALM 139:11-12

Night time can be scary for some of us. When the lights go out, our minds start thinking about all sorts of things. It's the time when we sometimes imagine monsters in the cupboards! Or it's when all our worries catch up with us and seem bigger than ever. Darkness can feel really dark.

But how incredible is it that the darkness is just the same as the light for God! He sees everything, he's never scared, and he doesn't sleep. Not only that, but his light is so powerful that it extinguishes darkness!

Think of any areas in your life that feel dark or shadowy and take some time to tell the Lord about them today in your journal.

TODAY I'M THANKFUL FOR...

1.
_____

2.
_____

3.
_____

_____

_____

_____

_____

_____

_____

_____

_____

_____

_____

_____

_____

_____

NOAH'S FACT

Humans spend a third of their life asleep, however cats spend two thirds of their life asleep.

Take a torch and shine a light onto your page of shadows. As you do it, speak this prayer over them: 'Lord Jesus, I declare that you will shine your light over these areas of my life that are dark and shadowy. Thank you that darkness is as light to you and that you love to bring things into the light. Thank you that Jesus is that light and through him I can be free of the darkness.'

Day 5

YOU ARE HIS MASTERPIECE

Take a look at God's masterpiece

For you created my
inmost being;
 you knit me together
in my mother's womb.
I praise you because
I am fearfully and
wonderfully made;
 your works are
wonderful,
 I know that full well.

PSALM 139:13-14

You are fearfully and wonderfully made! You are God's masterpiece, because you are a piece made by the master. There is nothing ordinary, nothing typical about you. You were made in God's image. You are a miracle and God is so delighted with his work.

Often we forget just how many miraculous and incredible things are going on in our bodies, Even before we were born our fingerprints were forming, our hearts were beating, we were learning to yawn, to cry and to stick out our tongues. The way God has made you is absolutely wonderful! Today, write about what it means to be created uniquely and perfectly by the Lord.

TODAY I'M THANKFUL FOR...

1.
_____

2.
_____

3.
_____

_____

_____

_____

_____

_____

_____

_____

_____

_____

NOAH'S FACT
Human ears never stop growing!

_____

_____

_____

_____

_____

_____

_____

Look in the mirror today and spend time examining your face. Look at your eye colour, the shape of your nose, your teeth, your smile. And now think about some of your qualities and your gifts. Remember that you are a child of the king. Declare over yourself: 'I am God's masterpiece! I am fearfully and wonderfully made!'

Day 6

SEEN

You may have heard it said before that God loves you too much to leave you as you are. Part of God knowing us and loving us is that he wants to change us.

He sees those parts of us that we often want to hide – our worries, our habits and our bad choices. In fact, sometimes we don't even see those bits of ourselves! We need God to show us what's going on deep inside.

As you write today, ask God to bring into your mind any anxieties – or 'offensive ways' as the psalmist says – that he wants to help you change. Write a prayer asking God to search you and lead you.

TODAY I'M THANKFUL FOR...

1.
_____

2.
_____

3.
_____

Search me, God, and
know my heart;
 test me and know
my anxious thoughts.
See if there is any
offensive way in me,
 and lead me in the
way everlasting.

PSALM 139:23-24

_____

_____

_____

_____

_____

_____

_____

_____

_____

_____

_____

_____

_____

_____

NOAH'S FACT

Hair and bone marrow are the two fastest things that grow in the human body.

Think about one thing you could change in your life today to either bring you closer to God, or make you healthier, or less anxious. Maybe you could give something up or do something extra – go for a run, stop eating sweets, set aside some time to pray, do something kind for your brother or sister or friend, get some more sleep, or sing some worship songs. Ask God to lead you and show you what to do.

Day 7

I TURN MY THOUGHTS TO GOD

Me and my BIG God brain!

How precious to me are your thoughts, God!
How vast is the sum of them!
Were I to count them, they would outnumber the grains of sand –
when I awake, I am still with you.

PSALM 139:17-18

What does it mean to you to 'turn your thoughts to God'? How can you make God's thoughts your thoughts?

Write down in your journal today what you imagine some of God's thoughts are. Think about Jesus and the things he spoke about, or the things he taught us about God. Jesus gives us so many clues about what God is like.

Imagine what God might be thinking as he looks at our world right now, or at the universe, or at you.

TODAY I'M THANKFUL FOR...

1. _____

2. _____

3. _____

_____

_____

_____

_____

_____

_____

_____

_____

_____

_____

_____

_____

_____

_____

_____

NOAH'S FACT

Your brain as a computer could hold two-and-a-half million gigabytes – that's the same as 300 years of solid TV shows!

Instead of praying your 'wishes' or 'dreams' today, why not take a few minutes to ask God how you can bring your thoughts in line with his thoughts. Instead of praying, 'Lord, help me win at football,' maybe he would rather you prayed, 'Lord, help me play my best game,' or, 'Lord, help me to be skilled and kind today.' Praying prayers in line with his thoughts is very powerful!

Well done on completing Week 4: Masterplan!
Never forget that you are fearfully and wonderfully
made by God. He knows you inside out – in fact,
no-one loves you like he loves you: totally, purely,
unconditionally. He's watching over you as you
sleep and he's there when you wake. He is totally
for you and cares so much about who you are, who
you are becoming, and the life you live.

Most importantly, no-one else is like you – you are
unique! Never compare yourself to other people.
God has made you to be *you* and, if you follow him,
you will grow to be a blessing to the world!

THINGS I'VE LEARNED ABOUT GOD THIS WEEK

_____

_____

_____

_____

_____

_____

THINGS I'VE LEARNED ABOUT ME THIS WEEK

_____

_____

_____

_____

_____

_____

_____

SALVATION PRAYER

Use this prayer or write your own version if you'd like to give your life to Jesus:

Thank you God that you made me.
Thank you Jesus that you died on the cross for me.
I know I have made mistakes.
I turn away from everything I know is wrong.
I ask for your total forgiveness.
Thank you for loving me completely.
Today I choose to put my faith in you.
I choose to follow you Jesus.
Please come into my life and fill me with your Holy Spirit.
Amen

Tell someone else if you have prayed this prayer. They would love to celebrate with you and to pray for you!

Printed in Great Britain
by Amazon

77982417R00047